STRING

SCULPTURE

John Winter

CREATIVE PUBLICATIONS, INC.

To Kennie

without her help this book would never have been completed

Creative Publications, Inc.
P. O. Box 10328
Palo Alto, California 94303

ISBN: 0—88488—016—8

10.074.6

PREFACE

String Sculpture is not a new form of art. Most school children have drawn simple designs using straight lines in their mathematics classes. It intrigues them that curved envelopes can be produced from straight lines. Even young children enjoy marking points on lines and connecting the points to discover the patterns which are created.

This art form has now come out of the classroom and into the home as beautiful objects d'art. The large variety of coordinated colors available in thread and yarn has helped kindle this new interest. Three dimensional designs made from acrylic plastic can produce striking conversation pieces or can be functional designs such as the lamp shown on the front cover. Several companies sell kits or finished products in both two and three dimensional designs. They are available in hobby shops and some department stores.

This book starts with very simple two dimensional designs and progresses to more complex designs. Step by step instructions are given for constructing two separate three dimensional designs — one made with wood and thread and the other constructed with acrylic plastic and monofilament fishing line. The final section gives patterns and winding instructions for several different string sculptures.

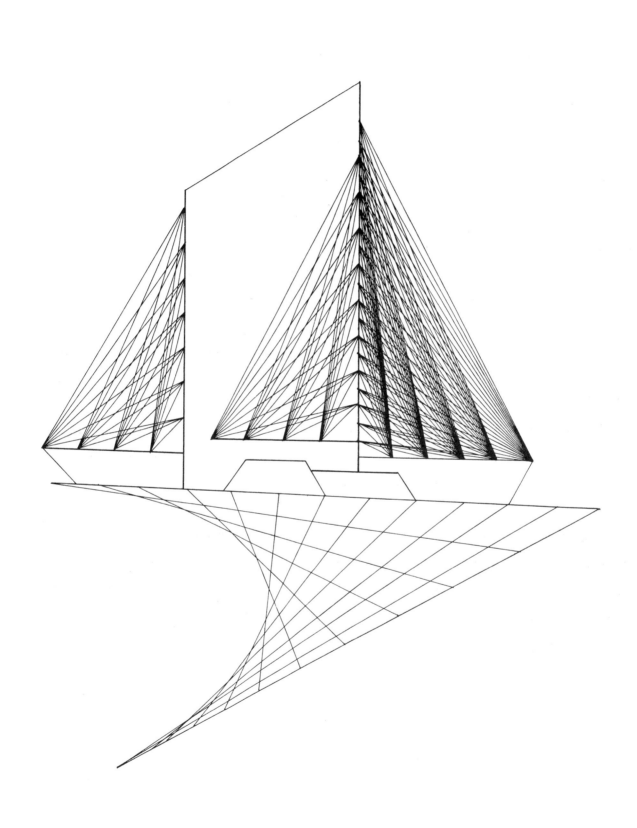

TABLE OF CONTENTS

PRINCIPLES INVOLVED IN STRING SCULPTURE

String sculptures are intriguing designs made entirely with straight lines and can be as simple or as complex as you wish. Some of the most complex looking designs are actually the easiest to create. To learn the fundementals of construction, try starting with the simpler patterns, then turn your imagination loose.

The basis of string sculpture is to stretch string between two points, thereby forming a straight line. By combining many stretched string segments you can produce aesthetically pleasing patterns and designs.

Simple geometric figures are often used as the basic outline with equally spaced points marked off along each edge. String is stretched between these points in a well defined order. The envelope (outermost edge or surface) of the straight line segments forms a surface which seems to be curved. By changing the "rule" by which points are connected together, you can alter the envelope which is produced. These curves can be two dimensional or three dimensional depending on the design which is employed.

Although there are mathematical principles involved in designing geometric string sculptures (drawing straight lines, circles or ovals and measuring lengths and angles) you don't have to be a mathematican to enjoy creating these interesting forms. Even though string sculptures are formed by stretching string (of various colors) between points, it is most convenient to use pencil and paper to design your final pattern. In this way it is easy to make corrections in your plan to obtain the most pleasing results.

TWO DIMENSIONAL DESIGNS

Two Straight Lines As The Basic Outline

The simplest form of design is constructed by connecting equally spaced points on two straight lines. These lines can be either intersecting or non-intersecting and the points can have either the same spacing or different spacing on the two lines.

Intersecting lines produce angles which can be used to form interesting curved envelopes. Several examples are shown below using the basic construction method of connecting point 1 with 1', point 2 with 2', etc. It is easy to imagine what curves would be produced by using other angles and lengths of lines.

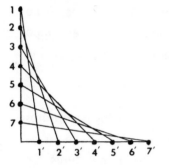

Right Angle
Equal Spacing

Acute Angle
Equal Spacing

Obtuse Angle
Equal Spacing

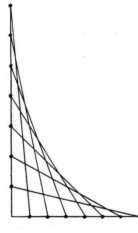
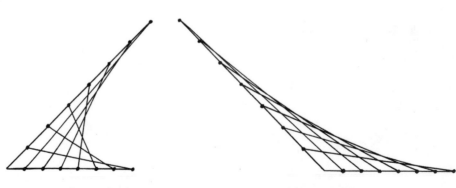

Right Angle
Unequal Spacing

Acute Angle
Unequal Spacing

Obtuse Angle
Unequal Spacing

Non-intersecting lines can produce essentially the same envelopes but without the sharp point of the angle. This is not as pleasing a design when it stands alone but may be useful in some composite designs. The examples below use the same angles and point spacing as those on the previous page. Only the "rule" by which points are connected has been changed. The two points closest to the intersection of the lines have been eliminated, thus producing a different envelope from the same basic design.

Right Angle
Equal Spacing

Acute Angle
Equal Spacing

Obtuse Angle
Equal Spacing

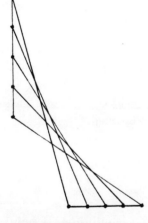

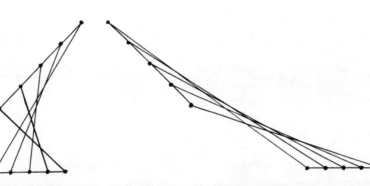

Right Angle
Unequal Spacing

Acute Angle
Unequal Spacing

Obtuse Angle
Unequal Spacing

This composite is composed of an intersecting line design together with a non-intersecting line design. Note that some of the points are used in both designs.

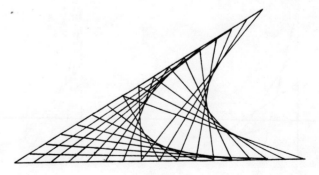

Parallel lines do not produce curved envelopes, but they might create interesting patterns in conjunction with other forms. Notice that equal spacing produces an intersection point half way between the parallel lines, while with unequal spacing the intersection point moves toward the more closely spaced line.

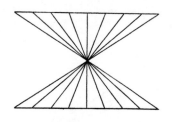

Parallel Lines
Equal Spacing
Centered

Parallel Lines
Equal Spacing
Offset

Parallel Lines
Unequal Spacing
Centered

Parallel Lines
Unequal Spacing
Offset

The "fullness" of a design depends on how many points are used on a given length line. If only a few points are used, the envelope does not form a smooth curved surface, while if too many points are used the separate lines are not distinguishable over much of the area.

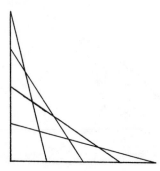
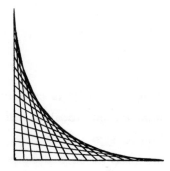

Three lines can be connected to form a triangle and points marked off on this outline. There are many ways of connecting lines between these points to produce different envelopes. A few of the possibilities are shown below. These are geometric composites since they use a geometric form and have multiple envelopes.

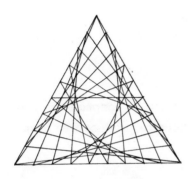
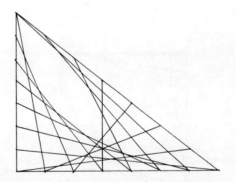
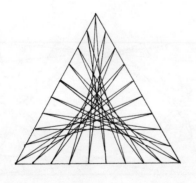
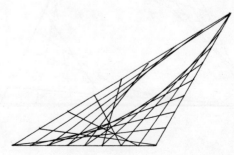
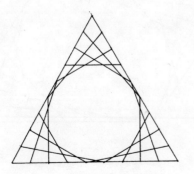

Another three sided geometric composite uses three equal length lines intersecting at a point to form three 120 degree angles.

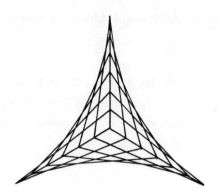

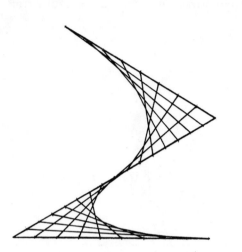

Three lines can be connected in many different combinations to produce free-form composites.

Any number of lines can be connected to form a closed polygonal outline. Four sides can produce a square or rectangle, rhombus or trapezoid.

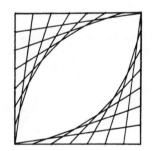

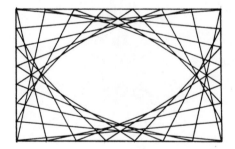

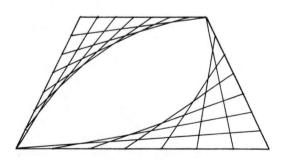

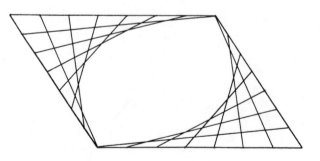

Five or more sides will produce higher order geometric figures. An example of a 24-sided, regular (equal lengths and angles) polygon is illustrated below.

Free-form composites may be made using any number of lines in infinite varieties. The only limitation is your own imagination.

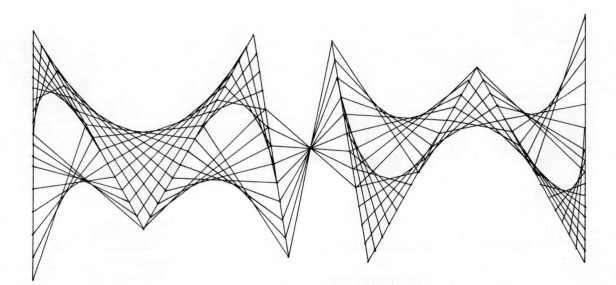

A Straight Line and a Circle as the Basic Outline

There are only a few basic combinations which can be produced by using a straight line and a circle. A straight line, or its extension, will either intersect the circle, be tangent to the circle, or not intersect the circle. Several examples of each possibility are shown below.

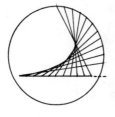 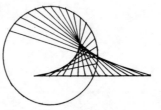

Intersecting

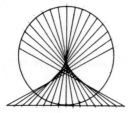 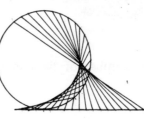 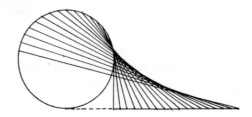

Tangent

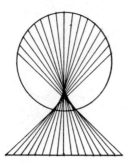 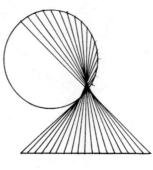 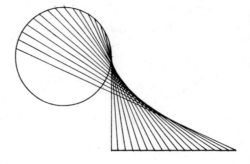

Non-intersecting

Circles (or Portions of Circles) as the Basic Outline

Some of the most intricate and interesting two dimensional designs can be made by using circles (or portions of circles). Equally spaced marks are constructed by "stepping off" equal lengths with a compass or by measuring equal angles with a protractor.

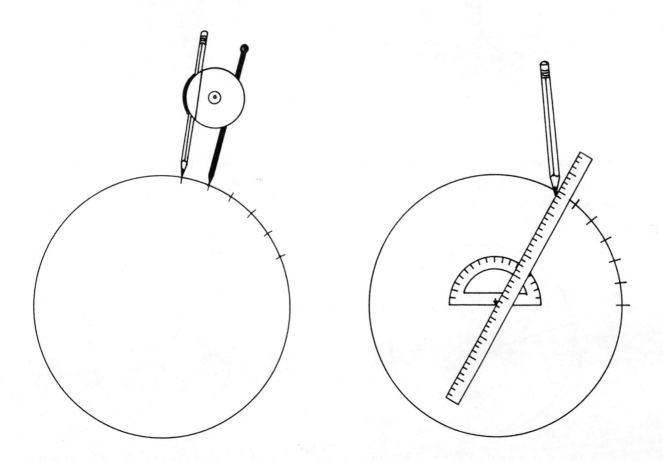

Examples using intersecting arcs of circles are shown below.

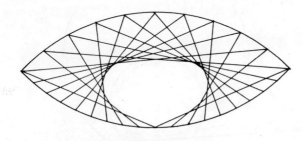

Unequal Spacing

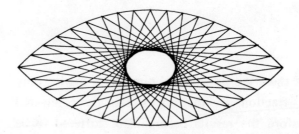

Equal Spacing

A small circle could be used with an arc of a larger circle.

Another possibility is to use a small circle within a larger circle. If there are an equal number of marks around both basic circles (equal angles), connecting the points can produce a circular envelope inside the small basic circle.

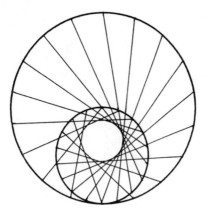
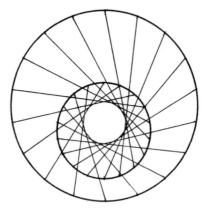

If there are an unequal number of marks, only a fraction of the marks can be connected before the results become too cluttered to be attractive or have an interesting form.

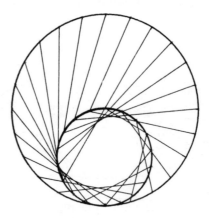

Many of these designs are the result of trial and error. Often only a few out of many attempts produce pleasing results. One simple design which always yields good results is a single circle with lines connecting points on the circumference. If a protractor is placed in the center of the circle and equal angles are marked off, these angles will intersect the circumference producing equal spaces around the circle.

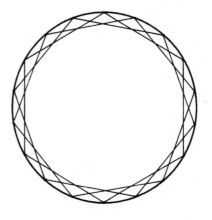

If lines are drawn by skipping 3 spaces between connected points as shown in the figure, the resulting envelope is a circle a little bit smaller than the basic circle. If 4 spaces are skipped, a smaller circle results. Skipping more and more spaces produces smaller and smaller circles.

The examples below show a circle divided into 18 equal spaces. The first example skips 8 spaces and produces a small envelope. The next example has two designs within the same circle — one constructed by skipping 8 spaces and the other by skipping 6 spaces. String sculptures using

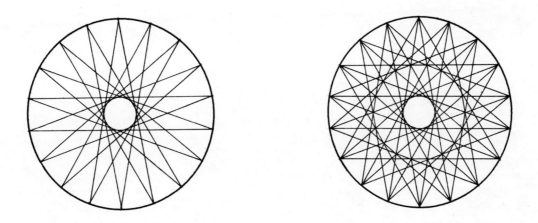

multiple designs within a circle are very dramatic if different colors of thread are used for each succeeding envelope. (See the front cover and Figures A and C on the back cover.) By using colored pencils to draw your pattern, you can get an idea of how the completed string sculpture will appear. In constructing a multiple layer design the smallest circle should be wound first; otherwise the succeeding layers would obscure the envelopes beneath them.

If the protractor is offset from the center of the circle, the resulting intersections from equal angle markings will produce unequally spaced points around the circumference. Drawing lines between these points will produce ovals within the circle which will be offset from the center as shown in the example below.

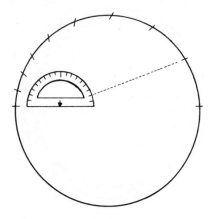
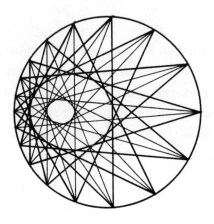

An Ellipse (Oval) as the Basic Outline

Previously described methods of designing circular string sculptures can also be used for elliptical designs. If an ellipse is substituted for the circle, pleasing variations in the basic outline occur and different types of envelopes can be produced.

An ellipse can be constructed by using two thumbtacks, a piece of string with the ends tied together, and a pencil. The thumbtacks are pushed into a stiff piece of construction material and the closed piece of string passed around them. A pencil is inserted inside of the closed string and the string stretched. By using the pencil to keep the string taut and moving the pencil around the thumbtacks, an ellipse is drawn. The pencil has a tendency to slip out of the loop and the string will stretch varying amounts depending on the tension applied by the pencil. A bit of practice will allow you to overcome these difficulties.

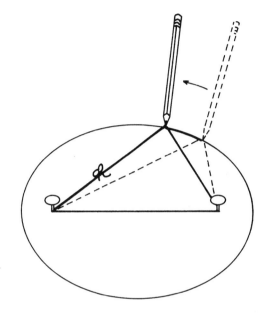

An elongated ellipse is produced if the thumbtacks are spaced far apart. As the thumbtacks are brought closer together, the ellipse becomes more circular.

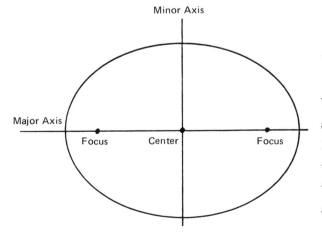

The point where a thumbtack is inserted is a *focus* of the ellipse. The *major axis* is the long dimension passing through the center and the two *foci*. The *minor axis* passes through the center and is perpendicular to the major axis. (See figure at left.)

If a protractor is placed at the center of the ellipse and equal angles are marked off, the envelope produced by connecting variously spaced points passes through an interesting progression. The smaller envelopes are ovals with their major axes perpendicular to the major axis of the basic outline. A circle is produced when points 90 degrees apart are connected. Ovals with their major axes in the same direction as the basic outline are created when fewer spaces are skipped. This design can be made very dramatic by using different colors for the various envelopes as illustrated on the front cover.

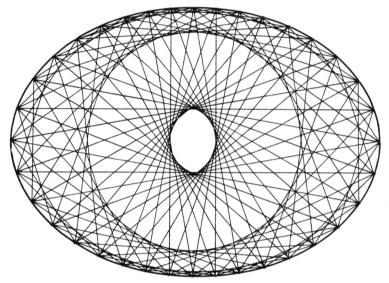

A less complex looking, more symmetrical design can be produced by stepping off equal spaces around the circumference of an ellipse with a compass. This is a trial and error method to find the correct compass spacing for an exact number of points around the circumference. The resulting envelopes for this construction will all have their major axes in the same direction as the original ellipse.

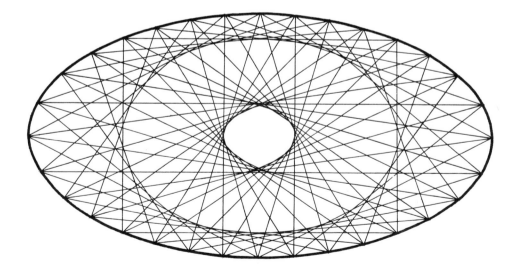

If a protractor is placed at the focus of the ellipse and equal angles marked off, an offset pattern will result with the smaller envelopes looking like circles and the larger envelopes becoming ovals. The centers of these envelopes start at the focus and move toward the center of the original ellipse. This is the design shown in Figure C on the back cover.

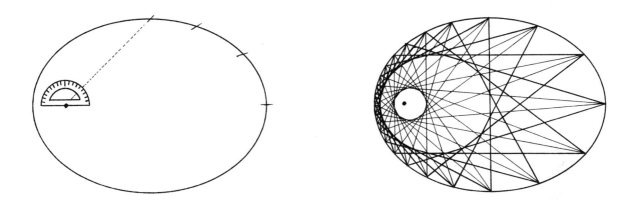

The protractor can be placed at other points within the ellipse with varying results. In the figure below the protractor is slightly offset from the focus toward the center and is slightly above the line of the major axis. This example is also shown in color as Figure A on the back cover. With a little imagination this could look like a fish. The addition of some "fins", constructed by using straight-line designs, enhances this image.

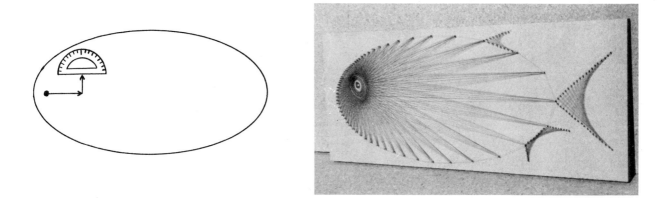

With a bit on ingenuity, a wide variety of string sculptures can be created by combining the forms presented in this book.

CONSTRUCTION MATERIALS FOR TWO DIMENSIONAL STRING SCULPTURES

The simplest materials to use in working out designs are a pencil and paper. The resulting designs can be suitable for framing and hanging just as they are. The next step in making these preliminary designs more pleasing to the eye is to use a variety of colored pencils to draw them.

Scratch board (or scraper-board) which is available from most art supply stores, is made of heavy cardboard with a coating which will scratch away. Where it is scratched with a sharp instrument, a contrasting color is revealed. A design drawn on this stiff board is ready for hanging.

SCRATCH BOARD

Thread comes in a rainbow of colors and can be very effectively used. The thread has to be stretched to produce a straight line, so a stiffer material than paper must be used. Cardboard construction paper (poster board, railroad board) which comes in a variety of colors can be used for the background. Still stiffer material such as plywood or pressed fiberboard can be painted or stained to give the desired color. Velvet or other cloth can be stretched over a board to produce a rich background texture. Holes can be punched or drilled through the board at the points used for straight line connections. The thread is pulled through these holes with a needle or crochet hook. It is pulled taut and then fastened to the back of the material with glue, tape, or by winding around nails or thumbtacks.

If wood or fiberboard is employed, an easier method is to drive brads or finishing nails at the desired points on the front of the board. The thread is tied to one nail and stretched to a nail the desired number of spaces away from the first one. The thread is wound around the second nail and stretched an equal number of spaces to the third nail. This process of skipping a certain number of spaces is continued until you return to the starting nail. There may be some nails which were not used during this winding sequence. If this occurs the string must be tied off and a new (unused) nail should be used as a beginning point and the process should be repeated until the entire envelope has been completed. (If an even number of nails is used around the circumference, you will *always* have to tie off the string more than one time.) A different color could be selected for the second envelope, etc. until the desired pattern is completed. As mentioned previously, the smallest envelope should be constructed first. For an example of a painted fiberboard string sculpture, see Figure A on the back cover which used ¾ inch brads for the points.

In winding a circular or elliptical thread sculpture it is possible to construct your points so that the thread has to be tied off only at the beginning and the end of the envelope. (When you get back to the starting nail the entire envelope will be completed.) This will *always* happen if the number of points around the circumference is a *prime number*. To assist in the construction of this type of design, a list of the equal angles needed for all prime number divisions between 5 and 100 is provided in the table on the next page. The angles start at $0°$ and stop just prior to $180°$. To complete the markings the protractor should be turned around and the reverse scale used to mark off the remaining points from $0°$ to $-180°$ using the numbers from the table a second time.

Several examples of circular designs using prime number spacing are shown on the pages following the table. Each design has the smallest two envelopes filled in. (Similar envelopes would be produced if an ellipse were used in place of the circle.) Note that as more points are used around the circumference, the lines more completely fill the circle. When a large number of points is used, very interesting effects are produced with only a few envelopes filled in (see examples N=37 and N=59 on page 29 which have only two envelopes completed). Small circular thread sculptures should use a small number of points and large designs should use many points.

Sewing thread is too small to show up well on large wall hangings, but colored yarn can be used very effectively. Burlap comes in many colors and is an excellent background material for use with yarn. The burlap is stretched tight on its frame with the pattern drawn on its back side. The yarn is threaded through from the back, stretched to form the line connecting two points on the front, threaded through to the back, and continued. Figure B on the back cover is an example of this method of construction.

	N=5	N=7	N=11	N=13	N=17	N=19	N=23	N=29	N=31	N=37	N=41	N=43
1	0.0	0.0	0.0	0.0	0.0	0.0	0.0	0.0	0.0	0.0	0.0	0.0
2	72.0	51.4	32.7	27.7	21.2	19.0	15.7	12.4	11.6	9.7	8.8	8.4
3	144.0	102.9	65.5	55.4	42.4	37.9	31.3	24.8	23.2	19.5	17.6	16.7
4		154.3	98.2	83.1	63.5	56.9	47.0	37.2	34.8	29.2	26.3	25.1
5			130.9	110.8	84.7	75.8	62.6	49.7	46.5	38.9	35.1	33.5
6			163.6	138.5	105.9	94.8	78.3	62.1	58.1	48.6	43.9	41.9
7				166.2	127.1	113.7	93.9	74.5	69.7	58.4	52.7	50.2
8					148.2	132.7	109.6	86.9	81.3	68.1	61.5	58.6
9					169.4	151.6	125.2	99.3	92.9	77.8	70.2	67.0
10						170.6	140.9	111.7	104.5	87.6	79.0	75.4
11							156.5	124.1	116.1	97.3	87.8	83.7
12							172.2	136.6	127.7	107.0	96.6	92.1
13								149.0	139.4	116.8	105.4	100.5
14								161.4	151.0	126.5	114.1	108.8
15								173.8	162.6	136.2	122.9	117.2
16									174.2	145.9	131.7	125.6
17										155.7	140.5	134.0
18										165.4	149.3	142.3
19										175.1	158.0	150.7
20											166.8	159.1
21											175.6	167.5
22												175.8
23												
24												
25												
26												
27												
28												
29												
30												
31												
32												
33												
34												
35												
36												
37												
38												
39												
40												
41												
42												
43												
44												
45												
46												
47												
48												
49												
50												

PRIME NUMBER TABLE FOR N EQUAL ANGLES

	N=47	N=53	N=59	N=61	N=67	N=71	N=73	N=79	N=83	N=89	N=97	
1	0.0	0.0	0.0	0.0	0.0	0.0	0.0	0.0	0.0	0.0	0.0	1
2	7.7	6.8	6.1	5.9	5.4	5.1	4.9	4.6	4.3	4.0	3.7	2
3	15.3	13.6	12.2	11.8	10.7	10.1	9.9	9.1	8.7	8.1	7.4	3
4	23.0	20.4	18.3	17.7	16.1	15.2	14.8	13.7	13.0	12.1	11.1	4
5	30.6	27.2	24.4	23.6	21.5	20.3	19.7	18.2	17.3	16.2	14.8	5
6	38.3	34.0	30.5	29.5	26.9	25.4	24.7	22.8	21.7	20.2	18.6	6
7	46.0	40.8	36.6	35.4	32.2	30.4	29.6	27.3	26.0	24.3	22.3	7
8	53.6	47.5	42.7	41.3	37.6	35.5	34.5	31.9	30.4	28.3	26.0	8
9	61.3	54.3	48.8	47.2	43.0	40.6	39.5	36.5	34.7	32.4	29.7	9
10	68.9	61.1	54.9	53.1	48.4	45.6	44.4	41.0	39.0	36.4	33.4	10
11	76.6	67.9	61.0	59.0	53.7	50.7	49.3	45.6	43.4	40.5	37.1	11
12	84.3	74.7	67.1	64.9	59.1	55.8	54.2	50.1	47.7	44.5	40.8	12
13	91.9	81.5	73.2	70.8	64.5	60.8	59.2	54.7	52.0	48.5	44.5	13
14	99.6	88.3	79.3	76.7	69.8	65.9	64.1	59.2	56.4	52.6	48.2	14
15	107.2	95.1	85.4	82.6	75.2	71.0	69.0	63.8	60.7	56.6	52.0	15
16	114.9	101.9	91.5	88.5	80.6	76.1	74.0	68.4	65.1	60.7	55.7	16
17	122.6	108.7	97.6	94.4	86.0	81.1	78.9	72.9	69.4	64.7	59.4	17
18	130.2	115.5	103.7	100.3	91.3	86.2	83.8	77.5	73.7	68.8	63.1	18
19	137.9	122.3	109.8	106.2	96.7	91.3	88.8	82.0	78.1	72.8	66.8	19
20	145.5	129.1	115.9	112.1	102.1	96.3	93.7	86.6	82.4	76.9	70.5	20
21	153.2	135.9	122.0	118.0	107.5	101.4	98.6	91.1	86.7	80.9	74.2	21
22	160.9	142.6	128.1	123.9	112.8	106.5	103.6	95.7	91.1	84.9	77.9	22
23	168.5	149.4	134.2	129.8	118.2	111.5	108.5	100.3	95.4	89.0	81.6	23
24	176.2	156.2	140.3	135.7	123.6	116.6	113.4	104.8	99.8	93.0	85.4	24
25		163.0	146.4	141.6	129.0	121.7	118.4	109.4	104.1	97.1	89.1	25
26		169.8	152.6	147.5	134.3	126.8	123.3	113.9	108.4	101.1	92.8	26
27		176.6	158.7	153.4	139.7	131.8	128.2	118.5	112.8	105.2	96.5	27
28			164.8	159.3	145.1	136.9	133.2	123.0	117.1	109.2	100.2	28
29			170.9	165.2	150.4	142.0	138.1	127.6	121.4	113.3	103.9	29
30			177.0	171.1	155.8	147.0	143.0	132.2	125.8	117.3	107.6	30
31				177.0	161.2	152.1	147.9	136.7	130.1	121.4	111.3	31
32					166.6	157.2	152.9	141.3	134.4	125.4	115.0	32
33					171.9	162.3	157.8	145.8	138.8	129.4	118.8	33
34					177.3	167.3	162.7	150.4	143.1	133.5	122.5	34
35						172.4	167.7	154.9	147.5	137.5	126.2	35
36						177.5	172.6	159.5	151.8	141.6	129.9	36
37							177.5	164.1	156.1	145.6	133.6	37
38								168.6	160.5	149.7	137.3	38
39								173.2	164.8	153.7	141.0	39
40								177.7	169.1	157.8	144.7	40
41									173.5	161.8	148.4	41
42									177.8	165.8	152.2	42
43										169.9	155.9	43
44										173.9	159.6	44
45										178.0	163.3	45
46											167.0	46
47											170.7	47
48											174.4	48
49											178.1	49
50												50

PRIME NUMBER TABLE
(CONTINUATION)

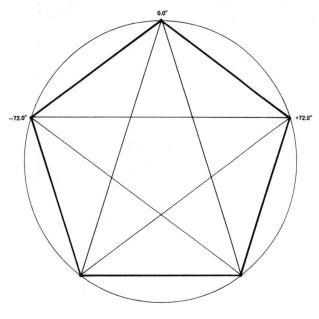

N=5

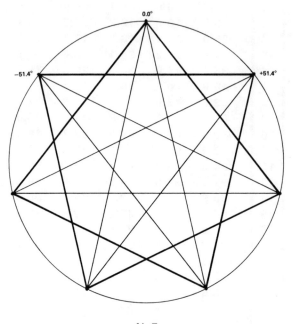

N=7

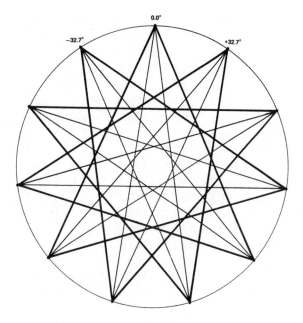

N=11

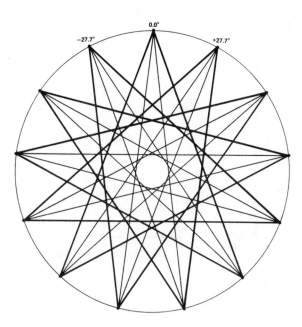

N=13

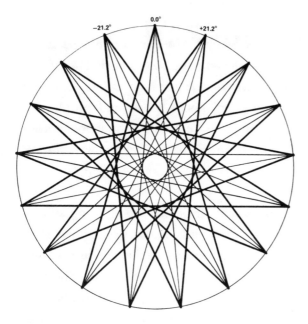

N=17

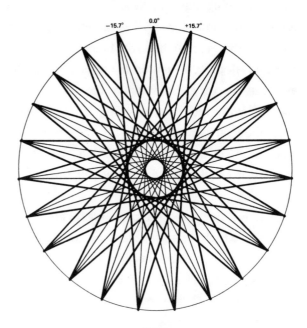

N=23

N=37

N=59

THREE DIMENSIONAL EFFECTS FROM TWO DIMENSIONAL DESIGNS

Long finishing nails or wood dowels can be used to give a three dimensional effect to designs which are composed of several envelopes (layers). The smallest envelope is wound around the pegs so that it touches the board. The second envelope is wound 1/4 inch up the pegs; the third envelope 2/4 inch up the pegs, etc. The form which is produced has a bowl-shaped appearance and can be very dramatic in the larger sizes with many different layers and colors. Consider starting with reds and working through oranges and yellows to greens, blues and purples for a rainbow effect as shown on the front cover. To construct this sculpture long wood dowels were used on a fiberboard backing. To create Figure C shown on the back cover, shorter dowels and fewer envelopes were employed for a shallower effect.

Shown on the opposite page are examples of three dimensional string sculptures using ellipses and one which uses a square as the basic outline. The elliptical designs use wood dowels of various diameters and heights to define the points on the basic outline, while the square uses finishing nails. The two elliptical string sculptures on the left use equal angle spacing; the protractor placed in the center for the top left figure and placed over the focus for the bottom left figure. The ellipse on the top right has equal spacing stepped off around the circumference.

Any two dimensional design which has multiple envelopes can be converted into a three dimensional design simply by spacing each succeeding envelope higher on the peg. Nails are easy to drive into a board but holes must be drilled in the board if dowels are used. Dowels must also be glued in their holes to prevent them from falling out. It is not easy to obtain uniform spacing between envelopes without either notching the pegs at the correct heights or using some form of spacer between envelopes.

The next section gives complete instructions for constructing a three dimensional design using wood dowels for the points. A simple spacing method to use between envelopes is also described.

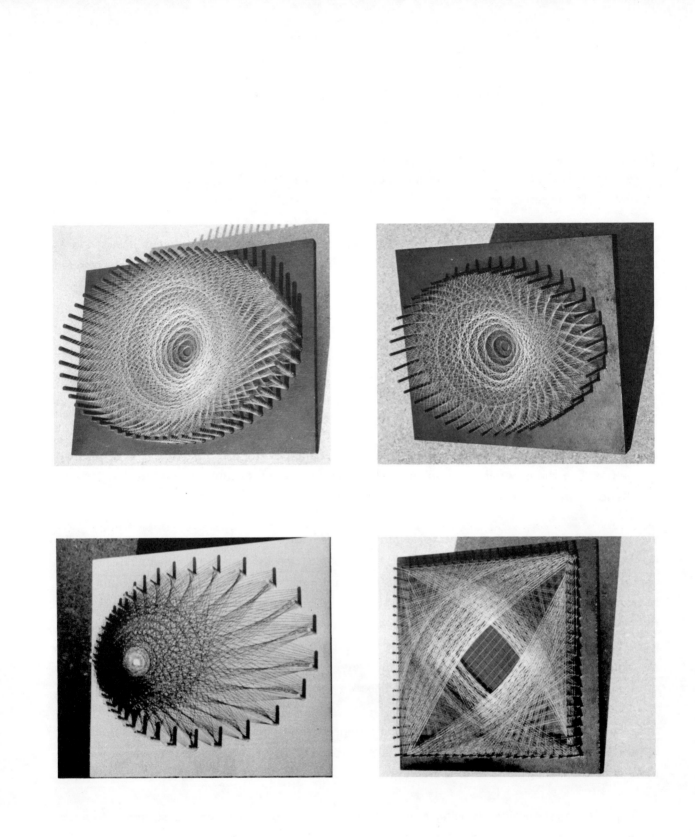

SAMPLE THREE DIMENSIONAL ELLIPSE AND WINDING INSTRUCTIONS

The photographs on the following page show the step by step procedure for constructing a three dimensional string sculpture using wood dowels. The first step is to draw the basic outline and mark off the points on suitable material (a shirt cardboard is shown in the example).

The basic outline shown in Step 1 is an ellipse (constructed using thumbtacks and string as described previously) with 43 equally spaced points around the circumference (constructed by stepping off with a compass — a trial and error process requiring small changes in the compass spacing until the exact number of points desired is produced after stepping off around the entire circumference). This pattern is taped to the board and a center punch or nail is used to mark through the pattern onto the board. (A pattern with 41 equally spaced points around an ellipse is presented on page 51.)

Step 2 shows an electric drill being used to drill holes at the points which have been marked on the board. The holes should be drilled completely through the board unless a drill press is used to obtain equal depth holes. Care should be taken to drill the holes perpendicular to the board so the pegs will stand up straight. A 1/8 inch drill bit should be used for the 1/8 inch dowels to assure a tight fit so the dowels will not lean.

Pieces of 1/8 inch dowel are cut to length and glued into the holes as shown in Step 3. The length of the pegs should be the depth of the hole plus the height of the design. This example uses a 9 x 12 x 5/8 inch piece of pressed fiberboard with dowels sticking 2½ inches out of the board (close to the maximum height allowable to prevent bending of the 1/8 inch dowels when the string is stretched). Therefore the 43 dowels were cut to 3-1/8 inch lengths. Glue is put into the hole, the dowel is inserted, pushed down as far as it will go and given several twists to distribute the glue. If the holes have been drilled completely through the board, the bottom should be on a smooth surface which will not be damaged by the leaking glue.

Spray paint is being used in Step 4 to give an appropriate background color. Since fiberboard is very porous and soaks up a lot of paint, it is desirable to paint it with a sealer before using the more expensive spray paint to give the desired color.

In Step 5 the first envelope is being wound. The thread is tied to one peg and stretched to a peg which is 21 pegs clockwise from the starting peg (count just less than ½ the total number of pegs for the smallest envelope — 43/2=21½). Wind the thread clockwise around this peg and stretch the thread taut. Count 21 pegs farther around and wind the thread clockwise around the new peg. Continue this process until you reach the starting peg again. Since 43 points is a prime number, the entire envelope will be completed when you return to this peg.

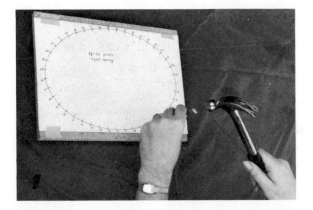

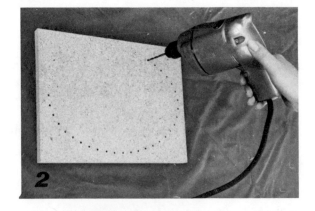

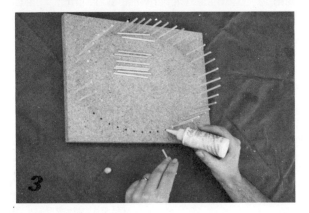

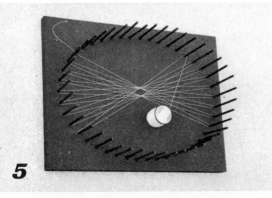

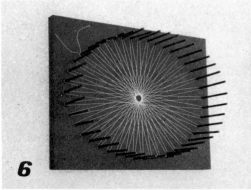

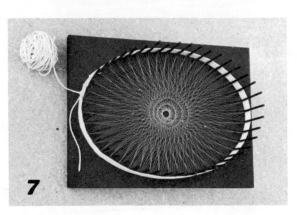

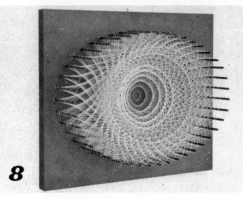

The completed first envelope is shown in Step 6. To finish the layer, the thread is wound clockwise around the starting peg and tied off while keeping the thread taut. The thread is pushed down on each peg until it touches the board.

Each succeeding envelope is wound by skipping one less peg than the preceding envelope. (The second envelope skips 20 pegs, the third envelope skips 19 pegs, etc.) Each new envelope should be started on a different peg to help conceal the tie-off knots. A simple method of spacing the layers is shown in Step 7 where several layers of heavy twine are wound around the pegs. This design uses four layers of twine between each envelope to space the envelopes ¼ inch apart.

The completed three dimensional string sculpture is shown in Step 8. It is composed of 11 envelopes; each one wound with a different color. (The maximum number of envelopes possible for this design would be 21.) After the winding has been completed, the spacing twine should be removed and white glue (which dries clear) should be painted over the string on each dowel to keep it from slipping up or down the peg.

THREE DIMENSIONAL STRING SCULPTURES USING INTERSECTING PLANE SURFACES

Two geometric figures can be connected to form intersecting planes. They produce striking string sculptures with the windings forming interesting curved envelopes in three dimensions. The most common way of joining these planes is at right angles. However, other angles can be used and more than two planes can be connected to form a single string sculpture. (See the hanging lamp on the front cover.)

The figure to the right shows a sculpture using two intersecting arcs of a circle as the upright figure and a circle as the intersecting plane in the middle of the design. It is reproduced in color on the front cover. A pattern and winding instructions for this design are presented on page 56.

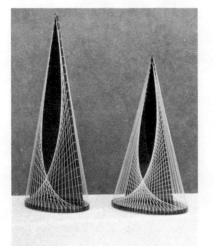

The string sculpture at the left uses an elliptical base with a triangle as the upright, intersecting surface. Two examples are shown here and are repeated in color as Figure D on the back cover. The dark smoked sculpture utilizes a triangle whose base is the same length as the major axis of the ellipse, while the green sculpture uses a triangle whose base is shorter than the major axis of the ellipse. Equal angles from the center of the ellipse are used to position the notches on the base and equal spaces are used on the sides of the triangle. The winding sequence is the same as the circle and triangle on page 52.

The photograph at the right shows a string sculpture using a triangle as the top and bottom portions of the upright, and a square for the horizontal, intersecting figure. It is also shown in color as Figure E on the back cover. A pattern and winding instructions are on page 54.

The construction material shown in these photographs is acrylic plastic. It is sold under a variety of trade names and is probably available at your local hobby shop. The figures are wound with monofilament fishing line. Colored thread could also be used but it does not produce as striking a finished product. Acrylic plastic string sculptures produce exceptionally beautiful designs, but there are other less expensive materials which are easier for the beginner to handle.

Since these designs are free-standing, considerably heavier material than paper must be used. Corrugated cardboard (from old packing cartons) is perhaps the easiest and least expensive material with which to begin. It is easily cut to the desired shape with scissors or a utility knife and the string can be wound in notches cut with a knife or hack saw. Almost any type of glue will hold the surfaces together and the cardboard can be painted before the winding is begun. The corrugated cardboard can be quite easily bent so some care should be exercised while handling and winding the design.

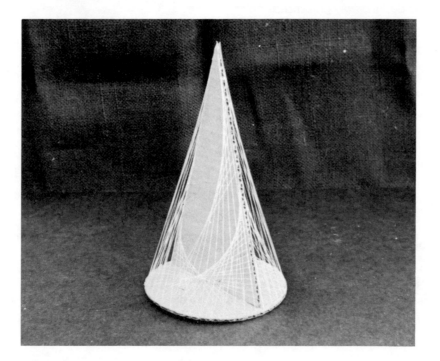

This example has two separate envelopes wound on the same form. To reproduce this design, use the pattern shown on page 52. Put twice as many notches in the bottom half of the triangle as are illustrated and follow the winding instructions using these closely spaced notches for the first envelope. The second envelope uses the normal spaces on the upper portion of the triangle. The winding is begun from the middle notch on the circular base to the first normally spaced notch on the triangle and completed in the customary manner.

Plywood, pressed hardboard, or masonite can be used for a sturdier finished product. However, a coping saw, jigsaw or sabersaw will be needed to cut along curved lines on these materials. These examples are made from masonite. The string sculpture on the left uses a square base with two triangles as the upright portions, but uses a winding sequence which is different from that used for Figure E on the back cover. The design on the right has a square base and uses the same winding sequence as described for a circular base on page 52.

The upright member might be made of thin strips rather than solid materials so that both the front and back windings are visible at the same time. The example on the left uses a rectangular base and a triangular upright member, both made from wood strips. The right hand figure uses a solid masonite elliptical base with a triangular upright made of masonite strips. Both sculptures use different winding methods for the front and back designs.

Acrylic plastic is the ultimate material to use for aesthetically pleasing string sculptures. It is available in clear (transparent), several colors of translucent and also in opaque colors. The transparent or translucent tones are more dramatic since the windings on the front and back sides can both be seen through the plastic material. Power tools are necessary to cut out curved lines and to buff the cut edges to a scratch-free, polished surface. Special glues are also needed to secure the planes together. Instructions for constructing an acrylic plastic string sculpture are given in the next section.

SAMPLE THREE DIMENSIONAL DESIGN USING A CIRCULAR BASE AND TRIANGULAR UPRIGHT

A pattern for producing this string sculpture, along with winding instructions, is presented on page 52. Circles and triangles are easy to modify to whatever size you desire. The example shown here is constructed with acrylic plastic, which presents some special problems not encountered with other materials.

Acrylic plastic comes with a protective paper covering on both surfaces to prevent scratching during the cutting processes. The pattern is drawn on this paper and the material is cut along this outline. Step 1 shows the circular base being cut out with a sabersaw. The base of the sabersaw has been screwed into the bottom of a piece of plywood with the blade sticking up through a small hole. The plywood is held solidly in place with C-clamps. This arrangement allows the use of both hands while guiding the plastic to cut along the outline. Hand tools could be used to cut along the curved surface, but this is a very time consuming process.

After the figures are cut out, the surfaces must be smoothed before they can be polished. If there are deep saw-tooth marks or flat spots on the curved surfaces, these must be removed with a file before the surfaces can be sanded. Step 2 shows the base of the triangle being sanded with medium grit sandpaper. This smooths the surface but leaves scratches which must be removed by using a very fine grit sandpaper.

All the sanded surfaces except the base of the triangle should next be buffed. The base of the triangle should *not* be polished since a slightly rough surface is necessary to assure a good bond when it is cemented to the circular base. Step 3 shows a ¼ inch electric drill with a buffing wheel. It is mounted in a drill press, but a drill holder (or another person holding the drill) would work just as well. A coarse buffing compound (pumice) is all that is needed to achieve a mirror-like polished surface. The buffing should be accomplished before cutting the notches along the edges. This keeps the buffing wheel from being frayed by the sharp edges of the notches and also eliminates cleaning buffing compound out of the notches before winding.

After the surfaces have been smoothed, sanded, and polished, a line should be drawn approximately 1/8 inch from the edge to serve as a gauge for the depth of the notches. This should not be marked at the same time you are drawing the pattern since the cutting and shaping process may not follow the outline exactly. The circle has 40 notches cut with equal spacing (9 degree increments) around its circumference, while the triangle has 20 equally spaced notches up each side. Step 4 shows a sabersaw being used to cut notches to the depth of the gauge line. An easy method of marking this line along curved surfaces is to use a compass with the point held against the outside surface and the pencil drawing the line.

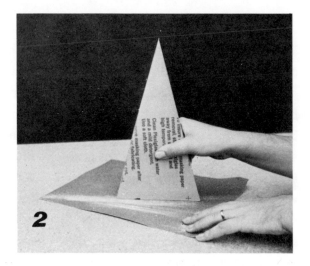

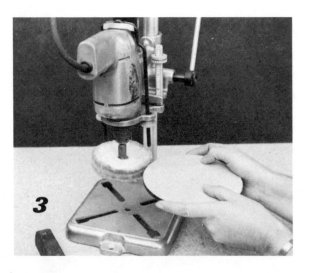

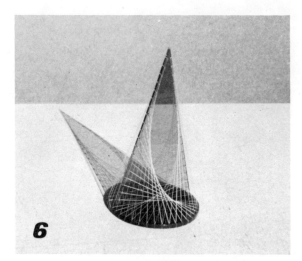

The geometric figures are now ready for cementing. The triangle should be centered on a diameter of the circle and held in a perpendicualr position. Step 5 shows an applicator being used to run a bead of cement along the base of the triangle. An eye dropper or artists paint brush could also be used, but the cement may attack the bulb of an eye dropper or dissolve the glue holding the bristles of a brush. The cement will be drawn under the base of the triangle by capillary action and cause a small amount of the acrylic to dissolve. (Cement will also be drawn up by the paper, so a small amount of the paper should be removed.) This causes the two surfaces to fuse together with a very strong bond. Most cements will form a weak bond in 10 to 30 seconds, with the bond becoming reasonably strong within 30 minutes. The cement and applicator are available at most stores carrying acrylic plastic material. Household cement will form a sufficiently strong bond for many applications since it contains acetone (which is a weak solvent for acrylics) or there are plastic glues on the market made for gluing acrylics and other forms of plastic.

Monofilament fishing line is used for the winding material. To start the winding, a large knot is tied in the line. This keeps the line from slipping through the first notch. Winding proceeds in the manner described on page 52. The completed string sculpture is shown in Step 6. Similar envelopes would be produced by substituting a square or an ellipse for the circular base as illustrated in the preceding section.

Non-uniform spacing along straight lines can produce variations in the basic design. One method shown below uses a progression for spacing points along one line where the first point has 1 unit of space between points, the second point has 2 units of space, etc. This same progression can be used for connecting points around a circle to give a *cardioid* envelope.

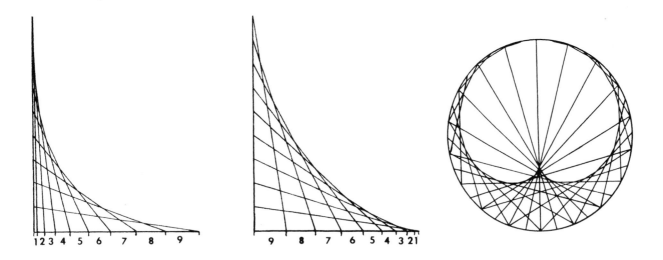

Another progression draws 1 line with 1 unit spacing, the next 2 lines with 2 unit spacing, etc. When this progression is used with a circle, the envelope becomes a spiral.

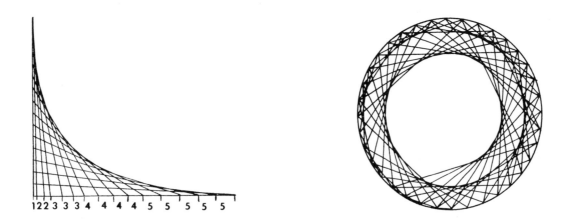

Cylinders can be used alone as shown in Figure F on the back cover with a spiral winding or in combination with plane surfaces as shown in the hanging lamp on the front.

Many other winding combinations are possible if cutting and threading the string from point to point is allowed instead of constraining the winding process to be continuous.

Free-form plane surfaces might be used instead of restraining the patterns to geometric designs, or a helical wire might be used with string stretched between marks on the wire.

String or yarn "pictures" can be made by outlining the picture with nails and winding a given color to cover the desired area. The winding doesn't have to proceed in any well defined order, just as long as the area becomes sufficiently filled with color. Almost any picture can be reproduced by filling in the background color first, then pounding in nails to outline a new section of color which can cover a portion of the first color, etc.

PATTERNS FOR MAKING STRING SCULPTURES

The patterns on the following pages are drawn on grid paper (graph paper). This is helpful in placing points on an ellipse, but straight lines and circles should probably be drawn with suitable instruments instead of plotting them from the grid. To make a string sculpture larger or smaller than is shown, a different size grid could be constructed. An easy way to do this is to draw points spaced ½ inch (or any desired spacing) along the top, bottom and sides of a plain piece of paper. Straight lines are drawn between corresponding points to create a grid. At the end

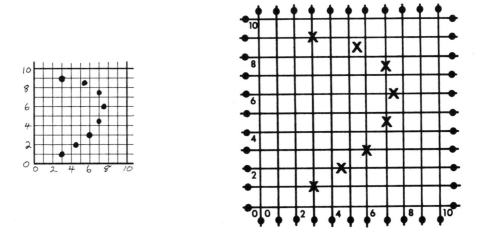

Original Pattern   New Grid for Enlarged Pattern

of this section there are two different scales of grid paper. One has 10 markings for each inch and the other has 10 markings for each centimeter. These can be reproduced and taped together to make larger grids. Also included are a grid with angular markings (polar co-ordinate paper) and a page with several protractors. These may be reproduced and used for marking off angles.

Winding instructions are given for each pattern. For construction hints and procedures see pages 32—35 and pages 38—40.

ELLIPTICAL FISH DESIGN — 47 POINTS

Similar to Figure A on Back Cover

This pattern uses an elongated ellipse for the body of the fish and intersecting lines for the tail and fins. There are 47 points (a prime number) around the ellipse which were constructed by placing a protractor over the position marked ⊠ and using angles from the table on page 27 under the column N=47. The eye of the fish will be at the position marked ⊠. A string sculpture made from this pattern should be at least twice as large as the size shown to avoid crowding of the pegs or nails close to the "eye." Smaller designs should use fewer points around the ellipse.

A suitable size grid should first be constructed. The points which are dots on the pattern are then transferred to this grid. The grid is taped to the board and nails are driven through the paper into the board at each point. The grid is then removed and the body of the fish wound. Next the points marked X are drawn on the grid (or constructed on the board directly with a ruler) and nails driven for the fins. These nails would be a hinderance in winding the body if they were driven prior to the winding. (The dots with circles around them are used in both the body and fin windings.) The last step is to wind the fins.

To wind the body the small "pupil" of the eye is wound first by tying the string to the nail at point 1, stretching the string counterclockwise (CCW) around nail 24, keeping the string taut and winding it CCW around nail 47, to nail 23, to nail 46, · · · · skipping 23 spaces each time. When you return to nail 1 the first envelope has been completed and the string should be tied and cut off. The second envelope might be wound in a sharply contrasting color. It is tied to nail 2, stretched to nail 24, to nail 46, to nail 21, · · · · skipping 22 spaces each time. The third smallest envelope starts on nail 3 and goes to nail 24 skipping 21 spaces, the fourth starts on nail 4 and goes to nail 24 skipping 20 spaces, etc. You may use as many envelopes as you desire and experiment with different colors for interesting effects. You might want to wind string from nail 1 to 2 to 3 to 4 · · · · to outline the body.

The winding of the fins is not as simple as drawing intersecting-line designs since a nail is not a point but has some width. For the top fin, the string should be tied to nail A and wound CCW around A' back to A; CCW around A to B; from B CCW around B'; CCW around B to C, etc. This gives two parallel lines between each point which are separated by the width of the nail. To finish the winding, thread should be stretched from A, touching the upper side of the fin nails to nail 5, touching the bottom side of the fin nails to nail 4, CCW around 4 and touching the upper side of the fin nails to 5, CCW around nail 5 and touching the bottom side of the fin nails to nail A. A similar procedure is used to wind the other fin and tail.

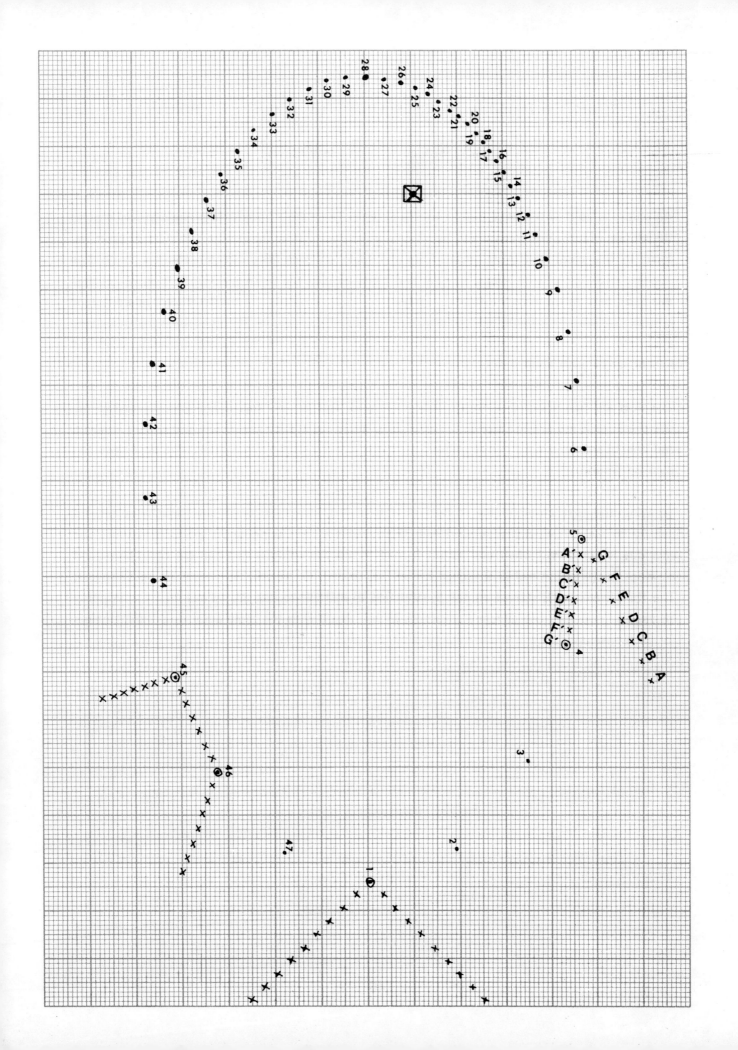

ELLIPSE WITH EQUAL ANGLES FROM THE FOCUS — 37 POINTS

Similar to Figure C on Back Cover

An ellipse is used as the basic outline in this pattern. There are 37 points (a prime number) around the ellipse which were constructed by placing a protractor over the position marked ⊠ (over the focus in this case) and using angles from the table on page 26 under the column N=37. The smallest envelope will be almost circular and centered over the point marked ⊠. You can change this basic pattern by using a different number of points or by placing the protractor at a different position within the ellipse. The basic outline of the ellipse can be obtained by simply drawing a smooth line connecting the points of the pattern on page 49. This pattern can be used full size or larger with good results.

The dots are first transferred to a suitable size grid (this size or larger). The grid is taped to the board and nails are driven through the paper into the board at each point. The grid is then removed and the board (and nails) spray painted with the desired background color. The envelopes can then be wound.

To wind the first envelope the string is tied to nail 1, stretched and wound clockwise around nail 19 to nail 37, clockwise around nail 37 to nail 18, · · · · skipping 18 spaces each time. The envelope is completed when you return to nail 1 and the string is tied and cut off. The second envelope is started on nail 2, stretched to nail 19, to nail 36, to nail 16, · · · · skipping 17 spaces. The third envelope is started on nail 3, stretched to nail 19, to nail 35, to nail 14, · · · · skipping 16 spaces. You may use as many envelopes as you desire with the same color or different colors for each envelope.

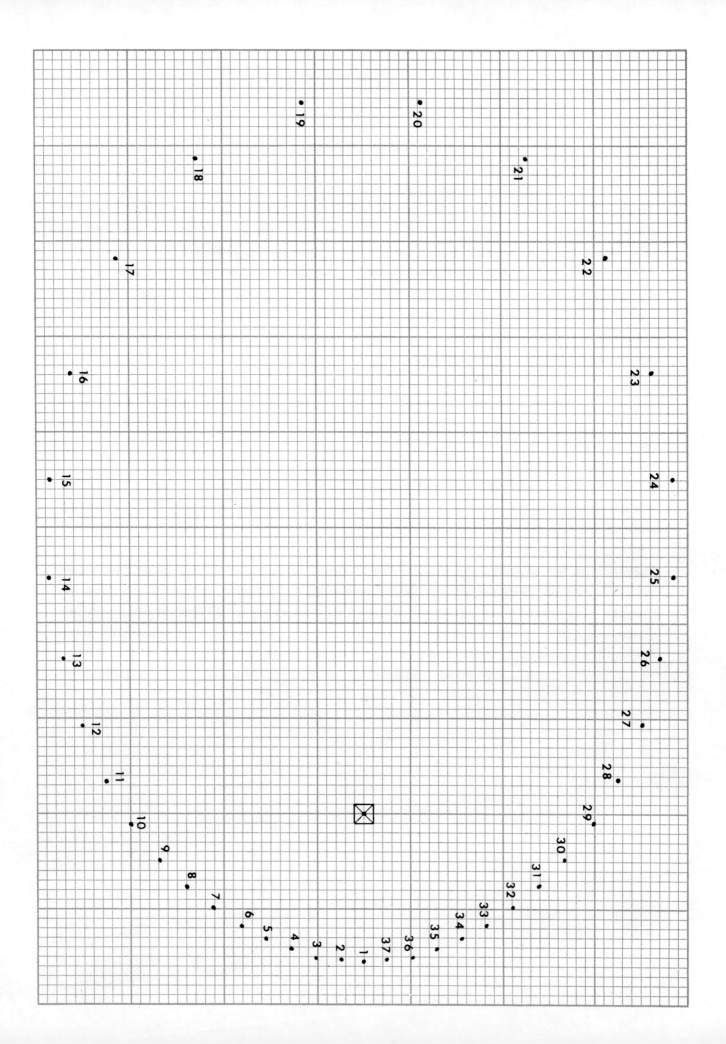

ELLIPSE WITH EQUAL ANGLES FROM THE CENTER — 59 POINTS

Lower Right on Front Cover

This pattern uses an ellipse as the basic outline. There are 59 points (a prime number) around the ellipse. These were constructed by placing a protractor in the center of the ellipse (marked ⊠) and using angles from the table on page 27 under the column N=59. The smallest envelope will be almost circular and as larger envelopes are wound the envelope becomes an oval with its major axis perpendicular to the major axis of the basic outline. The envelopes which skip 28 and 29 spaces are almost circular again with still larger envelopes producing ovals with major axes in the same direction as the major axis of the basic outline. This progression of envelopes can be seen in the photograph on the front cover and in the illustration on page 22.

The pattern has points spaced close enough together to allow you to draw a smooth curve connecting the points to form the basic ellipse outline. You can then construct your own points and position a protractor anywhere inside the ellipse.

To construct this design the dots are transferred to a grid at least twice as large as the pattern. The grid is then taped to the board and nails are driven through the paper into the board at each point. The paper is removed and the board (and nails) can be painted with the desired color.

To wind the first envelope the string is tied to nail 1, stretched and wound clockwise around nail 30 to nail 59, clockwise around nail 59 to nail 29, · · · · skipping 29 spaces each time. The envelope is completed when you return to nail 1 and the string is tied and cut off. The second envelope is started on nail 2, stretched to nail 30, to nail 58, to nail 27, · · · · skipping 28 spaces. The third envelope is started on nail 3, stretched to nail 30, to nail 57, to nail 25, · · · · skipping 27 spaces. You may use as many envelopes as you desire in any pleasing color combination.

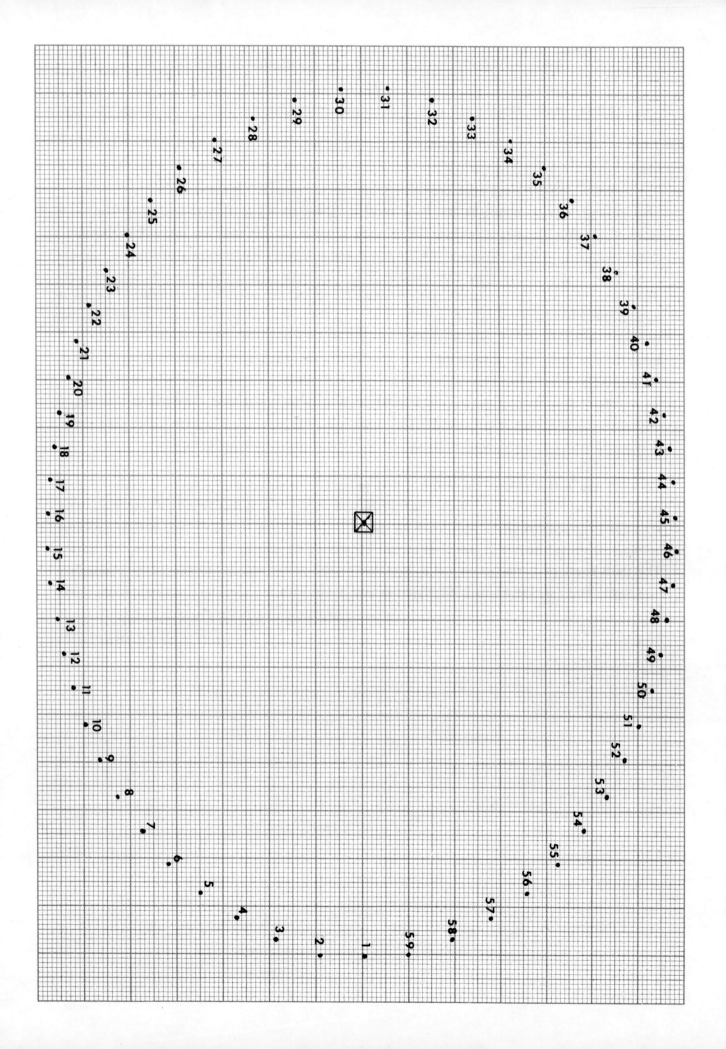

ELLIPSE WITH EQUAL SPACING AROUND CIRCUMFERENCE — 41 POINTS

Similar to Example on Page 33

This pattern uses an ellipse as the basic outline. There are 41 equally spaced points (a prime number) around the circumference. These were constructed by stepping off with a compass. The compass is set and, starting where the major axis intersects the outline, it is stepped halfway around the ellipse. There should be exactly 20½ (41/2) spaces going halfway around the ellipse. This means that the 20th space stepped off (point 21) should be the same distance below the major axis as the 21st space (point 22) is above the axis. The first trial will probably not produce the correct spacing, so the compass should be adjusted slightly and tried again. The envelopes will all be ovals with their major axes in the same direction as the major axis of the ellipse.

To construct this design the dots are transferred to a suitable size grid. The grid is then taped to the board and nails are driven through the paper into the board at each point. The paper is removed and the board (and nails) can be painted with the desired color.

To wind the first envelope the string is tied to nail 1, stretched and wound clockwise around nail 21 to nail 41, clockwise around nail 41 to nail 20, ···· skipping 20 spaces each time. The envelope is completed when you return to nail 1 and the string is tied off and cut. The second envelope is started on nail 2, stretched to nail 21, to nail 40, to nail 18, ···· skipping 19 spaces. The third envelope is started on nail 3, stretched to nail 21, to nail 39, to nail 16, ···· skipping 18 spaces. You may use as many envelopes as you desire with any pleasing combination of colors.

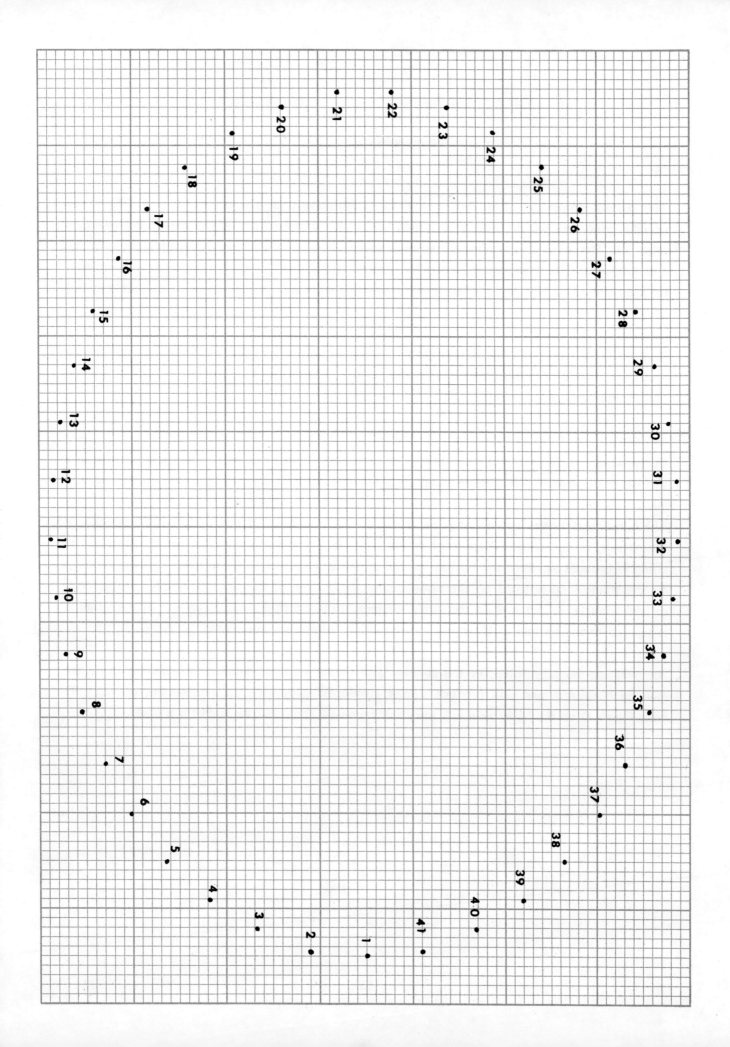

THREE DIMENSIONAL CIRCLE AND TRIANGLE

See Photographs on Page 39

This pattern produces a three dimensional string sculpture with a circular base and a triangular upright. Step by step procedures for constructing this pattern with acrylic plastic are given on page 38. The circular base has 40 equally spaced notches (9 degree increments) around the circumference. The triangle has 20 equally spaced notches (half as many notches as in the circle) on each side. The base of the triangle is somewhat smaller than the diameter of the circle in this design.

It is not recommended that this pattern be used directly since more accurate outlines can be produced with a compass, a protractor and a ruler. This also allows you to construct a string sculpture of any desired size.

To construct this design the circle and triangle are first cut out of a suitable rigid material and the notches cut. Next the circle is placed on a horizontal surface and the triangle is glued in a vertical position with the base centered on a diameter of the circle as indicated on the pattern.

The winding is begun by securing the string to the underside of the circle with tape, glue, a thumbtack, or by tying a large knot in the string which will not pull through the notch. The string is brought up from the bottom of the circle through notch 1, stretched through notch 2 on the triangle, to notch 3 on the circle, under the bottom of the circle to notch 4, to notch 5 on the triangle, to notch 6 on the circle, underneath to notch 7, · · · · . The end of the winding is secured to the bottom of the circle and the string sculpture is completed.

An oval can be substituted for the circular base (equal angle or equal length spacing both can give good results) and will produce similar envelopes. (Compare the photograph on page 39 with Figure D on the back cover.) A square or rectangle could also be used for a base.

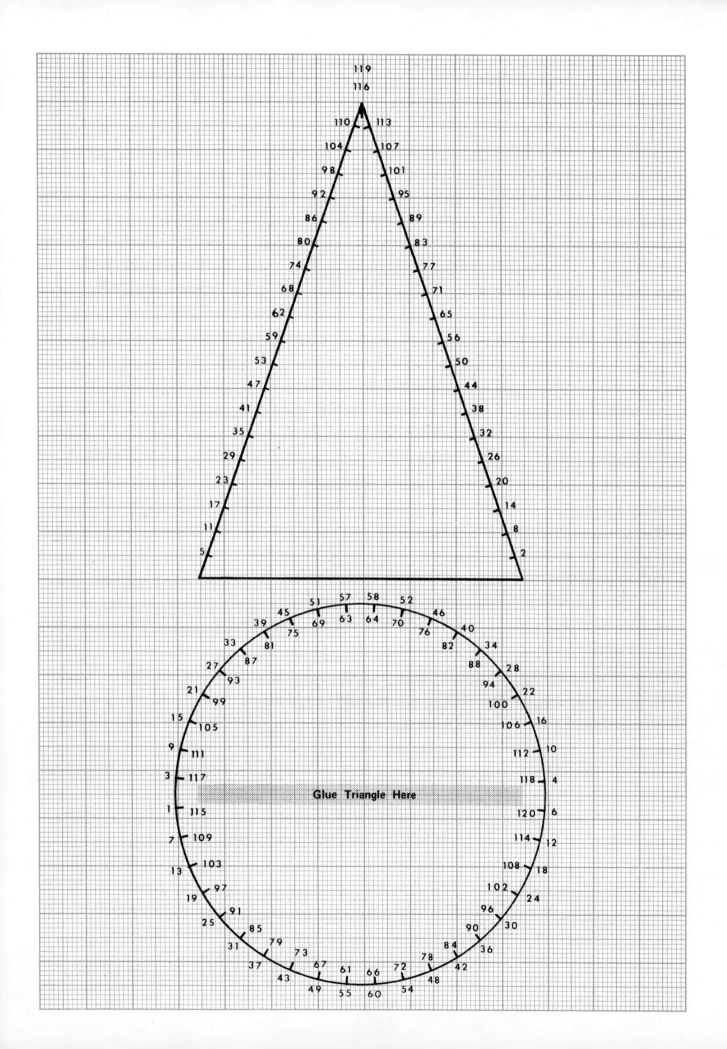

Glue Triangle Here

THREE DIMENSIONAL SQUARE AND TRIANGLES

Similar to Figure E on Back Cover

This pattern produces a three dimensional string sculpture which should be mounted on a pedestal base. The upright is constructed from two triangles and the horizontal plane figure is a square. The same number of equally spaced notches are cut along the edges of the square and the triangles. This pattern uses 11 notches along each edge, but any number can be used depending on the size of the sculpture you are constructing. (Figure E on the back cover used 15 notches.)

It is not recommended that this pattern be used directly since more accurate outlines can be produced with a ruler. This also allows you to construct a string sculpture of any desired size.

After the forms are cut out of a suitable rigid material and the notches are cut along the edges, the two triangles are glued to the top and bottom of the square as indicated on the pattern. The flat tip of the bottom triangle is used for mounting on the base. However, the string has to be wound through this notch before the tip can be glued on the base.

The envelope is wound by tying a large knot in the beginning of the string and pulling the string through the bottom of notch 1 on the square until the knot catches in the notch. The string is then stretched through notch 2 on the upper triangle, to notch 3 on the square, to notch 4 on the lower triangle, to notch 5 on the square, · · · · . After the string is wound through the last notch (128) it is tied around a nearby string (124) to prevent it from pulling back out of the notch. The string sculpture is then completed and ready for gluing to a square or rectangular base.

Triangles with a different height can be used to produce a string sculpture with different proportions. If you cut twice as many notches on the triangles as on the square, the winding sequence on page 52 can be used. The resulting envelope will be the same as shown in the photograph at the top of page 37.

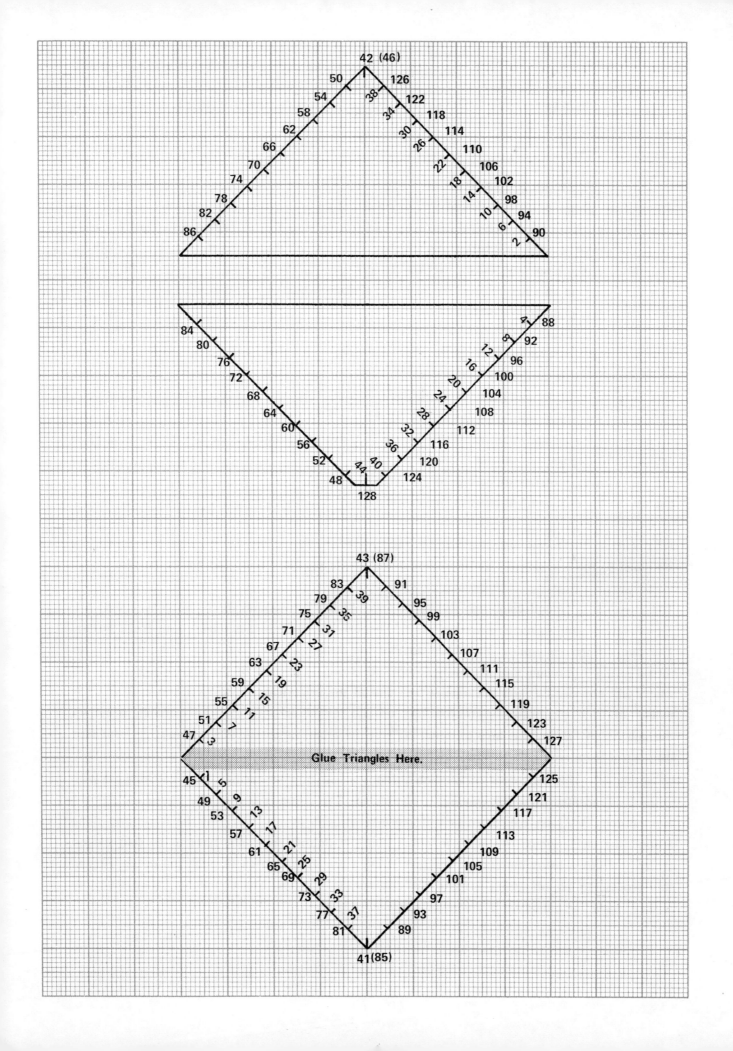

Glue Triangles Here.

THREE DIMENSIONAL INTERSECTING ARCS AND CIRCLE

Lower Left on Front Cover

This pattern produces a three dimensional string sculpture which should be mounted on a pedestal base. The upright portion is constructed from two intersecting arcs of a circle. Equal angle spacing from the center is used to position the notches. One end of the intersecting arcs is cut off for mounting on the base. This means that the equal angles for the notches cannot go to 90 degrees (the last notch in this design is at 66 degrees). A circle (divided into two semicircles) is used as the intersecting plane in the middle of the arcs.

It is not recommended that this pattern be used directly since much more accurate outlines can be produced with a compass and protractor. A large compass is needed for drawing the intersecting arcs or a thumbtack and piece of string can be used. The arcs are drawn first and then two semicircles are drawn with diameters equal to the width of the intersecting arcs. This design uses 12 equal angle spacings in a total of 66 degrees (5.5 degree increments) on the arcs and 12 equal angles in 90 degrees (7.5 degree increments) on the semicircles. If the arcs are cut off closer to the tip, allowing notches to be cut to 75 degrees, you can use 15 equal angle increments of 5 degrees on the arcs and 6 degrees on the semicircles.

After cutting the forms out of a suitable rigid material and cutting the notches, the semicircles are glued to the two sides of the intersecting arcs at the positions indicated on the pattern.

The envelope is wound using two strings at once. String 1 is wound in the notches labled with capital letters and string 2 is wound (simultaneously) in the notches labled with small letters. The two strings are wound alternately so that the design can be completed without having to thread string 2 through the previously completed (string 1) portion of the envelope. Large knots which will not slip through the notches are tied at the beginnings of strings 1 and 2. String 1 is pulled up from the bottom of notch "A" on the semicircle until the knot catches, stretched through notch "B" on the arcs to notch "C" on the other semicircle. While string 1 is kept taut (to keep it from falling out of the notches), string 2 is pulled up through notch "a", to notch "b", to notch "c". This procedure of winding string 1 a few notches farther, then catching up with string 2 is repeated until the winding is completed. The string is tied off by stretching string 1 from notch "VV" on the lower part of the arcs through notch "WW" on the circle and tying around the string which is already in notch "oo". A double knot may have to be tied around string "oo" to prevent the end of the taut string from slipping back through the notch. Repeat this process to tie off string 2 using the appropriate notches. The completed string sculpture is then ready for gluing on a square or rectangular base.

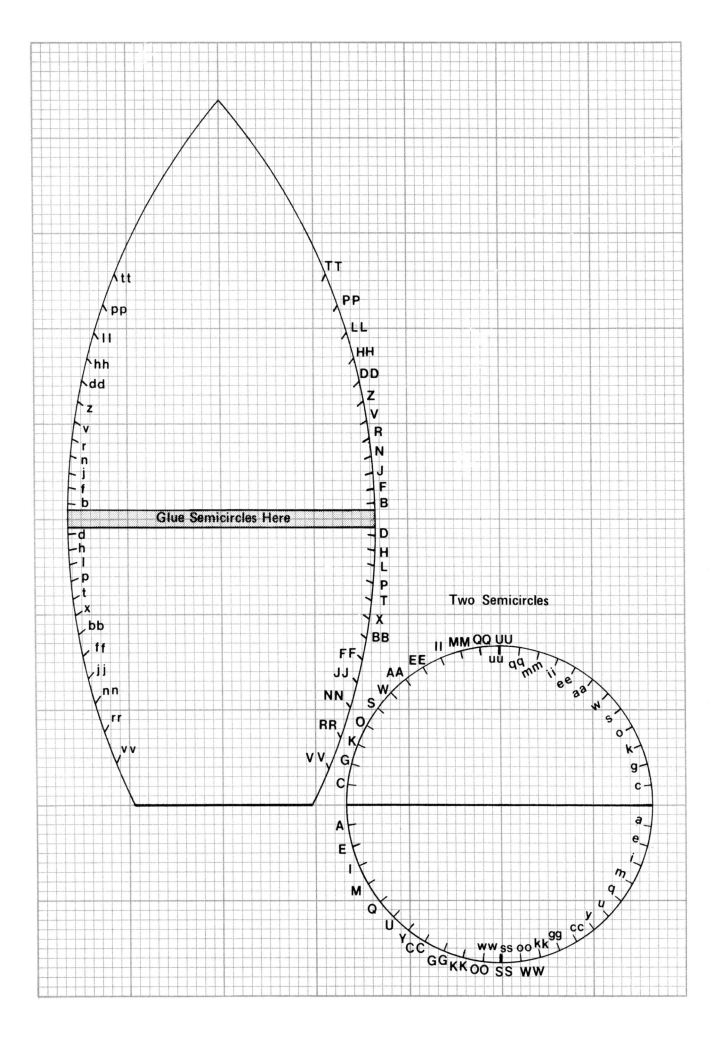

Glue Semicircles Here

Two Semicircles

LAMP WITH EIGHT TRIANGULAR VANES

Top Left on Front Cover

This design produces a lamp which has three dimensional windings on the eight triangular vanes. It is constructed with a 4 inch acrylic plastic cylinder to house the light fixture and bulb. The vanes are glued to the outside of the cylinder at 45 degree intervals. The lamp can either be mounted on a base for a pedestal lamp or can be made into a hanging lamp as shown on the front cover.

The pattern on the opposite page is drawn to half scale. The 4 inch diameter cylinder is cut to a 12 inch length and marked at 45 degree intervals. Triangles with 30 degree x 60 degree x 90 degree angles are used for the eight vanes. The hypotenuse is constructed 13 inches long to extend ½ inch above and below the cylinder. The short side of the triangle has 27 notches cut with ¼ inch spacing and the long side has 27 notches cut with 3/8 inch spacing. After cutting and notching the triangles, the vanes are glued onto the cylinder.

The envelopes are wound using two strings at once. String 1 is started by tying a large knot at the beginning and pulling it through notch "a" of vane 1 until the knot catches. It is wound in a clockwise direction around the cylinder to notch "A" on vane 2, to notch "a" on vane 3, to notch "A" on vane 4, · · · · . When you reach vane 8 the string should be secured in notch "A" so that string 2 can be started. String 2 is started in notch "a" on vane 2, wound in the opposite direction (*counterclockwise*) to notch "A" on vane 1, to notch "a" on vane 8, to notch "A" on vane 7, · · · · . When string 2 has passed through notch "A" on vane 3, it should be secured so that string 1 can be wound clockwise through the "b" and "B" notches. This procedure of winding string 1 clockwise through its lettered notches for one revolution, then winding string 2 counterclockwise through notches with the same letter is repeated until the envelope is completed. The string is then tied off and the lamp is ready for mounting.

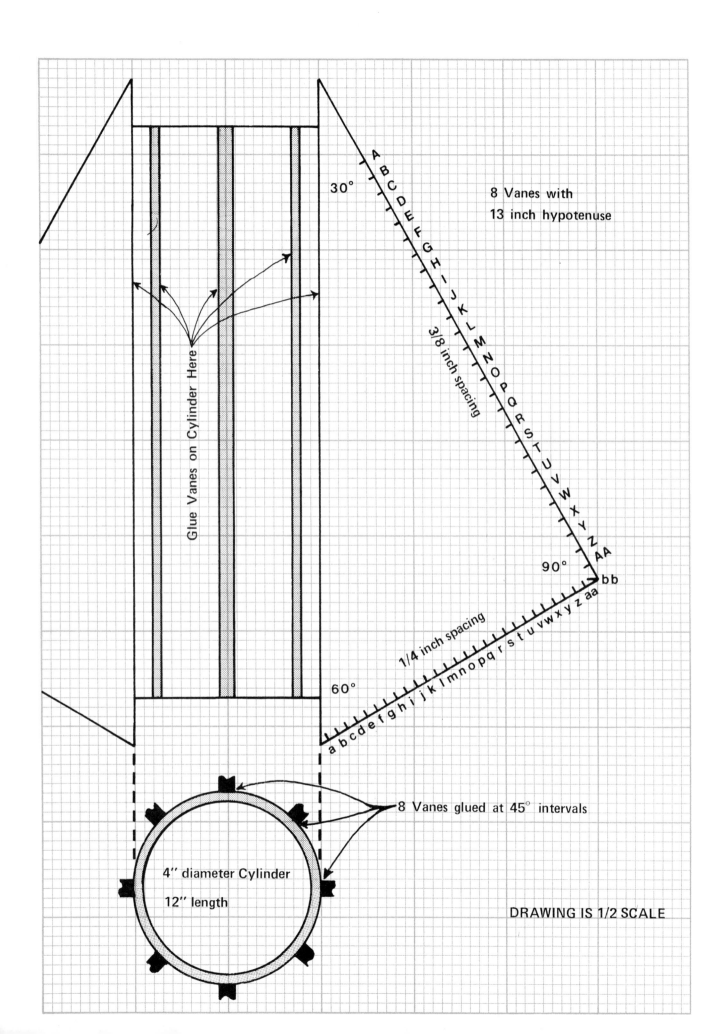

30°

8 Vanes with
13 inch hypotenuse

Glue Vanes on Cylinder Here

A
B
C
D
E
F
G
H
J
K
L
M
N
O
P
Q
R
S
T
U
V
W
X
Y
Z
AA

3/8 inch spacing

90°

bb

1/4 inch spacing

60°

a b c d e f g h i j k l m n o p q r s t u v w x y z aa

8 Vanes glued at 45° intervals

4″ diameter Cylinder

12″ length

DRAWING IS 1/2 SCALE

CYLINDER WITH SPIRAL WINDING

Similar to Figure F on Back Cover

The cylinder shown as Figure F on the back cover is made of acrylic plastic. Cardboard mailing tubes, plastic bottles and tin cans are other sources of cylinders. This design is the same as the two dimensional spiral presented in the lower figure on page 41, but has a three dimensional effect since the string is wound from notches on the top of the cylinder to notches on the bottom.

There are 72 notches (5 degree increments) along the top rim of the cylinder and an equal number along the bottom rim. The string is taped to the outside of the cylinder, stretched over the top rim through notch 1, down through the cylinder to notch 2 on the bottom rim (skipping 1 space), back up over the outside of the cylinder to notch 2 on top, down through to notch 4 on the bottom (skipping 2 spaces), up to notch 3, through to notch 5 (skipping 2 spaces), up to notch 4, through to notch 7 (skipping 3 spaces), · · · · . This process of winding the first line segment inside the cylinder with 1 space skipped, the next 2 segments with 2 spaces skipped, the next 3 segments with 3 spaces skipped, etc. is continued until the desired spiral winding is produced.

Other winding sequences can be tried with the notched cylinder to produce different envelopes. Another possibility would be to drill holes in the cylinder and thread the string through the holes with a needle.

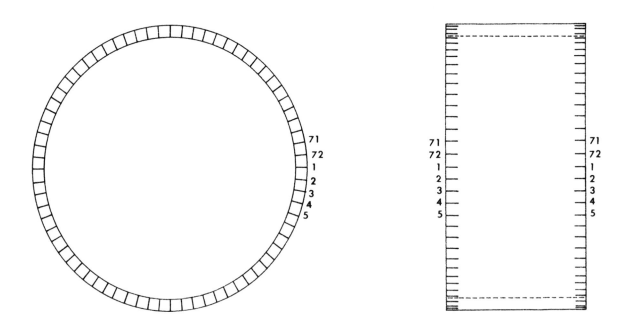

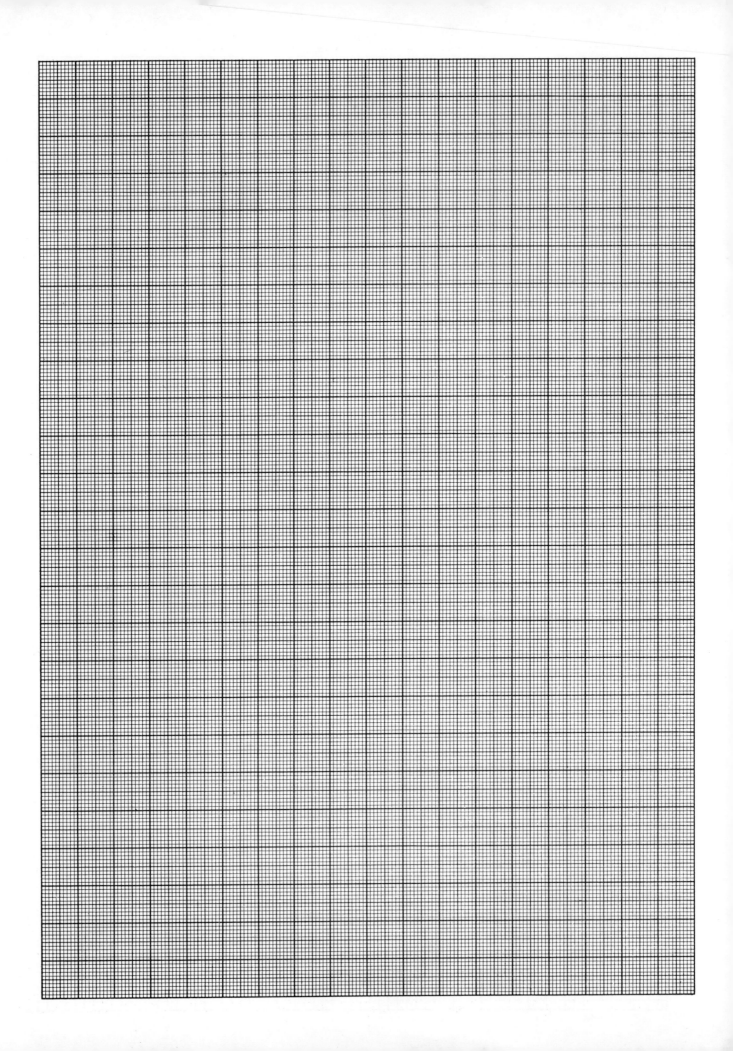

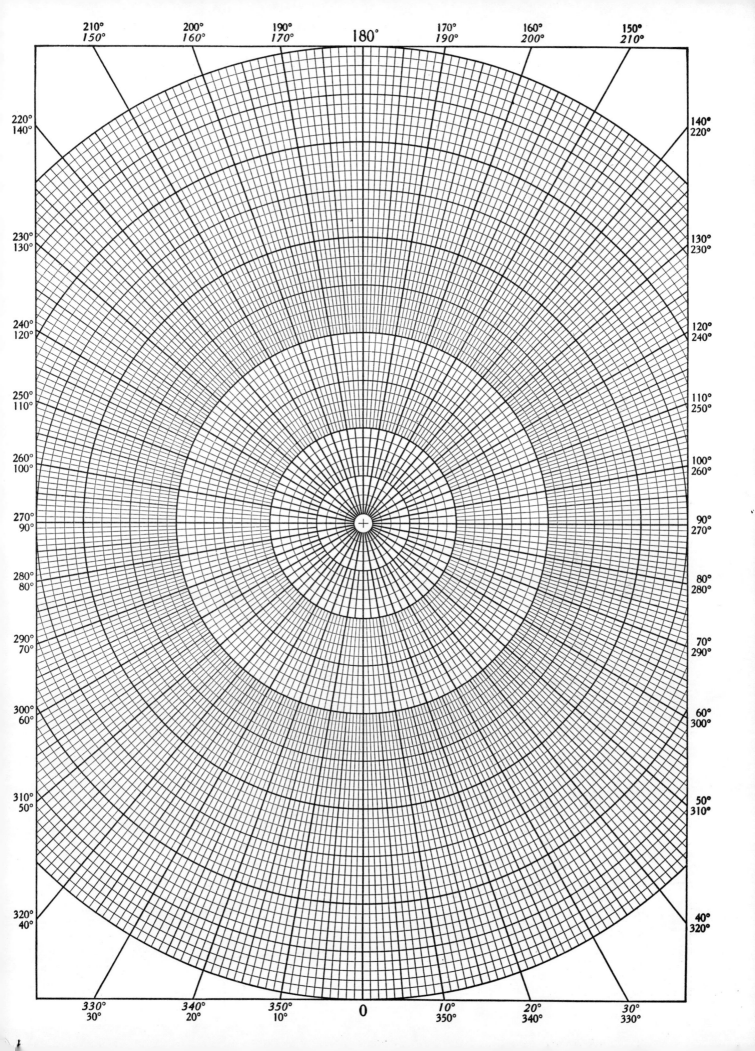

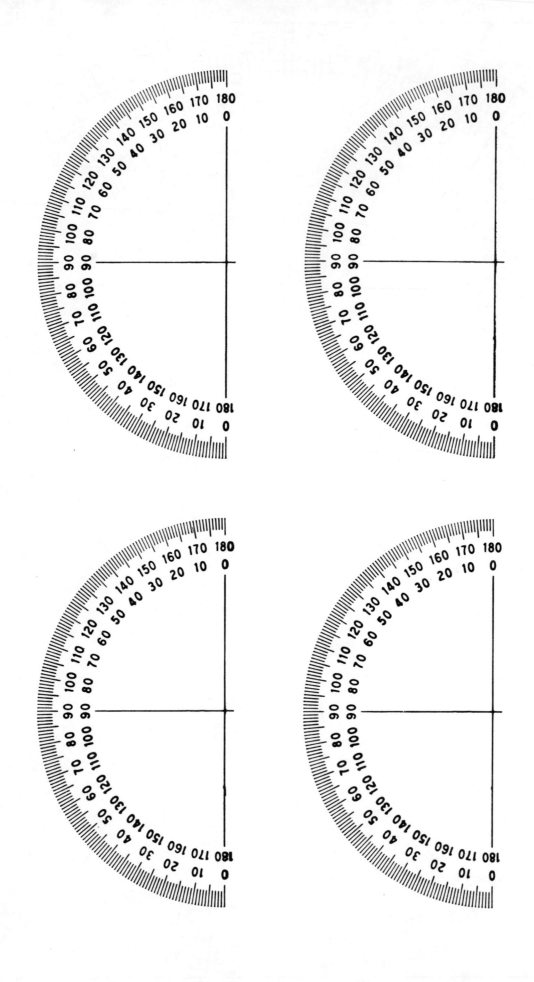